GW00371001

Valuing the Outdoors

the shared vision and values for outdoor play and learning in the early years

Jan White and Liz Edwards

OPENING
UP THE
OUTDOORS

 Early Childhood **Outdoors**

 **MUDDYFACES**

Jan White is co-founder and strategic director of Early Childhood Outdoors. She is author of the Core Values for Outdoor Play and editor of Outdoor Provision in the Early Years (Sage 2011).

Liz Edwards is founder and chief imaginer of Muddy Faces. She is author of Knife Use with Groups - a Forest School Leaders Guide and creator of the Outdoor Hub.

Copyright
Valuing The Outdoors text and images © Jan White and Liz Edwards (2018)

The text of the Vision and Core Values statements are copyright free, but please always acknowledge the source as 'Vision and Values Partnership and Learning through Landscapes (2004)'

Cover image by Menna Godfrey
Photographs © Carol Duffy, © Liz Edwards, © Vanessa Gilliam, © Menna Godfrey, © Vanessa Lloyd, © Vikki Palmer, © Ann Thompson, © Jan White

All rights reserved. No part of this publication may be reproduced, stored in a retrieval system or transmitted in any form, or by any means, electronic, mechanical, photocopying, recording or otherwise, without either permission in writing from the publisher or a licence permitting restricted copying.

Acknowledgements
Many thanks to the children, adults and settings who have so generously contributed images for this booklet, including Ann Thompson, Sian Rees-Jones & Bognor Regis Nursery School, Carol Duffy, Petra Arzberger & Children's Oasis Nursery, Sue Palmer & Farley Nursery Schools, Menna Godfrey & Quackers, Jane Harrison & Red Hen Children's Day Nursery, Suzanne Scott & Sandfield Natural Play Centre, Vanessa Gilliam, Vanessa Lloyd and Vikki Palmer.

Disclaimer
The contents of this publication have been provided to help increase the understanding and confidence of practitioners aiming to develop outdoor play with young children. As with any aspect of early years provision, it is always necessary to carry out ongoing benefit-risk assessment and management according to the specific children, situation and conditions pertaining.

The author, publisher and contributors cannot take any responsibility for the use of the guidance and ideas given, and cannot accept any legal responsibility or liability for any harm arising from the use of the guidance, resources and experiences presented in this publication.

Contents

1   The Opening Up The Outdoors initiative

3   Establishing beliefs about outdoor play

5   The Vision for all young children

Core Values:

7   •   Outdoors is essential
9   •   The critical role of play
11   •   Following children's interests
13   •   Adults are essential
15   •   The special nature of the outdoors
17   •   A responsive environment
19   •   Rich and real experiences
21   •   Long periods of time
23   •   Sufficient challenge, risk and safety
25   •   Outdoor play for everyone

27   The history of the Shared Vision and Values

28   Opening Up The Outdoors - providing ongoing support

OPENING UP THE OUTDOORS

Much has happened over the past decade in progressing the right of all young children to access play, and the learning that takes place through their play, in the outdoors. We now have a broad consensus across the UK and at all levels from Government to practitioners and parents, that outdoor play matters and that **'outdoor learning'** is important – and increasingly, that this is as significant as indoor learning. Along the way, many settings have been exploring their approach to outdoor play and learning, and several are pushing at the boundaries of what it really means to be in the outdoors, what kind of outdoor environment can be harnessed, such as woodlands and beaches, and in what ways the outdoors can be used for the benefit of young children. Exciting times are ahead for the field of outdoor play and learning!

However, many early years settings still have to work with difficult access to the outdoors, uninspiring outdoor spaces, restricted funds for design, resources, training, outdoor clothing and so on, staff who are early on in their own journey of working well with the outdoor environment, and parents who are not yet fully on board with the setting's intentions for learning outdoors. There is still much work to do! The outdoors has so much potential to offer to young children: **how can we unlock and open up this fabulous treasure trove?**

Opening Up The Outdoors builds on the remarkable success of Jan White and Liz Edwards' previous Mud Play initiative, which aimed to deepen the understanding, importance, value and range of experiences from mud play as continuous provision and to support practitioners to achieve this (Making a Mud Kitchen 2011). This larger initiative shares the vision and goal of *more children thriving outdoors, more often and for longer, benefiting from richer and more meaningful environments offering authentic, rewarding and satisfying experiences* through a long term, three cornered approach tackling the **WHY**, **WHAT** and **HOW** of really good outdoor play.

Establishing beliefs about Outdoor play

Valuing the Outdoors: the shared vision and values for outdoor play and learning in the early years

As always when developments take place and settings strive to do the best for their children and families, it is critical to bring into full awareness the reason for what we are doing and the values that underpin how we work upon it – and it is important that these values are shared by all involved. Establishing belief in the importance of *being* outside, trust that *learning* happens well in the outdoors, and commitment to increasing the *amount of time* and the *quality of experiences* children can access in the outdoor environment is a slow and long-term process that requires wide-ranging support, on-going energy and lots of small steps of success.

These shared beliefs and values act as the threshold to going outside for play, wellbeing and learning in the first place: the main **DOORWAY** between indoors and outside.

And adults - both educators and parents - are the **DOOR KEEPERS** who must open the door and keep it open as widely as possible, and resist circumstances that try to push it closed!

As the first and crucial step of addressing the **WHY** of outdoor play in the Opening Up the Outdoors initiative, **Valuing the Outdoors** re-launches the Shared Vision and Core Values for High Quality Outdoor Experiences for Young Children first created by the Vision and Values Partnership (supported by Learning through Landscapes) in 2004.

The Vision for all young children

* All children have the right to experience and enjoy the essential and special nature of being outdoors.

* Young children thrive and their minds and bodies develop best when they have free access to stimulating outdoor environments for learning through play and real experiences.

* Knowledgeable and enthusiastic adults are crucial to unlocking the potential of outdoors.

Outdoors is essential
giving it equal status, equal time and equal thinking to the indoors

Young children should be outdoors as much as indoors and need a well-designed, well-organised, integrated indoor-outdoor environment, preferably with indoors and outdoors available simultaneously.

Outdoor provision is an essential part of the child's daily environment and life, not an option or an extra. Each half of the indoor-outdoor environment offers significantly different, but complementary, experiences and ways of being to young children. They should be available simultaneously and be experienced in a joined-up way, with each being given equal status and attention for their contribution to young children's well-being, health, stimulation and all areas of development.

Outdoor space must be considered a necessary part of an early years environment, be well thought through and well organised to maximise its value and usability by children and adults, and design and planning must support developmentally appropriate practice, being driven by children's interests and needs.

The critical role of play

play outdoors as the medium and mechanism for wellbeing, learning and development

Play is the most important activity for young children outside.

Play is the means through which children find stimulation, wellbeing and happiness, and is the means through which they grow physically, intellectually, emotionally and socially. Play is the most important thing for children to do outside and the most relevant way of offering learning outdoors. The outdoor environment is very well suited to meeting children's needs for all types of play, building upon first-hand experiences.

Following Children's Interests
child-led experiences that are meaningful and worthwhile

Outdoor provision can, and must, offer young children experiences which have a lot of meaning to them and are led by the child.

Because of the freedom the outdoors offers to move on a large scale, to be active, noisy and messy and to use all their senses with their whole body, young children engage in the way they most need to explore, make sense of life and express their feeling and ideas. Many young children relate much more strongly to learning and teaching offered outdoors rather than indoors.

All areas of learning must be offered through a wide range of holistic experiences, both active and calm, which make the most of what the outdoors has to offer.

Outdoor provision needs to be organised so that children are stimulated, and able, to follow their own interests and needs through play-based activity, giving them independence, self-organisation, participation and empowerment. The adult role is crucial in achieving this effectively.

Adults are essential
the role of adults outdoors

Young children need all the adults around them to understand why outdoor play provision is essential for them, and adults who are committed and able to make its potential available to them.

Young children need practitioners who value and enjoy the outdoors themselves, see the potential and consequences it has for young children's wellbeing and development, and want to be outside with them. Attitude, understanding, commitment and positive thinking are important, as well as the skills to make the best use of what the outdoors has to offer and to effectively support child-led learning; the adult role outdoors must be as deeply considered as that indoors. Practitioners must be able to recognise, capture and share children's learning outdoors with parents and other people working with the child, so that they too become enthused. Cultural differences in attitude to the outdoors need to be understood and worked with sensitively to reach the best outcomes for children.

The special nature of the outdoors
capturing and harnessing the difference

The outdoor space and curriculum must harness the special nature of the outdoors, to offer children what the indoors cannot. This should be the focus for outdoor provision, complementing and extending provision indoors.

The outdoors offers young children essential experiences vital to their wellbeing, health and development in all areas. Children who miss these experiences are significantly deprived.

Outdoors, children can have the freedom to explore different ways of 'being', feeling, behaving and interacting; they have physical (up as well as sideways), mental and emotional space; they have room and permission to be active, interactive, messy, noisy and work on a large scale; they may feel less controlled by adults.

The real contact with the elements, seasons and the natural world, the range of perspectives, sensations and environments (multi-dimensional and multi-sensory), and the daily change, uncertainty, surprise and excitement all contribute to the desire young children have to be outside. It cannot be the same indoors, a child cannot *be* the same indoors - outdoors is a vital, special and deeply engaging place for young children.

A responsive environment

creating a dynamic, versatile and flexible environment

Outdoors should be a dynamic, flexible and versatile place where children can choose, create, change and be in charge of their play environment.

Outdoor provision can, and should, offer young children an endlessly versatile, changeable and responsive environment for all types of play where they can manipulate, create, control and modify. This offers a huge sense of freedom, which is not readily available indoors. It also underpins the development of creativity and the dispositions for learning. The space itself as well as resources, layout, planning and routines all need to be versatile, open-ended and flexible to maximise their value to the child.

Rich and real experiences irresistible contexts for exploration, talk and play

Young children must have a rich outdoor environment full of irresistible stimuli, contexts for play, exploration and talk, plenty of real experiences and contact with the natural world and with the community.

Through outdoor play young children can learn the skills of social interaction and friendship, care for living things and their environment, be curious and fascinated, experience awe, wonder and joy and become 'lost in the experience'. They can satisfy their deep urge to explore, experiment and understand and become aware of their community and locality, thus developing a sense of connection to the physical, natural and human world.

A particular strength of outdoor provision is that it offers children many opportunities to experience the real world, have first-hand experiences, do real tasks and do what adults do, including being involved in the care of the outdoor space. Settings should make the most of this aspect, with connected play opportunities.

An aesthetic awareness of and emotional link to the non-constructed, uncontrolled, multi-sensory and multi-dimensional natural world is a crucial component of human well-being, and increasingly absent in young children's lives. The richness of cultural diversity is an important part of our everyday world; this can and should be explored by children through outdoor experiences. Giving children a sense of belonging to something bigger than the immediate family or setting lays foundations for living as a community.

Long periods of time uninterrupted time, every day, throughout the year

Young children should have long periods of time outside. They need to know that they can be outside every day, when they want to and that they can develop their ideas for play over time.

High quality play outdoors, where children are deeply involved, only emerges when they know they are not hurried. They need to have time to develop their use of spaces and resources and uninterrupted time to develop their play ideas, or to construct a place and then play in it or to get into problem-solving on a big scale. They need to be able to return to projects again and again until 'finished' with them.

Slow learning is good learning, giving time for assimilation. When children can move between indoors and outside, their play or explorations develop further still. Young children also need time (and places) to daydream, look on or simply relax outside.

Sufficient challenge, risk and safety
feeling secure, becoming risk competent

Young children need challenge and risk within a framework of security and safety. The outdoor environment lends itself to offering challenge, helping children learn how to be safe and to be aware of others.

Children are seriously disadvantaged if they do not learn how to approach and manage physical and emotional risk. They can become either timid or reckless, or be unable to cope with consequences. Young children need to be able to set and meet their own challenges, become aware of their limits and push their abilities (at their own pace), be prepared to make mistakes, and experience the pleasure of feeling capable and competent. Challenge and its associated risk are vital for this. Young children also need to learn how to recognise and manage risk as life-skills, so as to become able to act safely, for themselves and others.

Safety of young children outdoors is paramount and a culture of 'risk assessment to enable' that permeates every aspect of outdoor provision is vital for all settings. Young children also need to feel secure, nurtured and valued outdoors. This includes clear behavioural boundaries (agreeing rules to enable freedom), nurturing places and times outside and respect for how individual children prefer to play and learn.

Outdoor play for everyone meeting the needs of individuals, taking an active part

Outdoor provision must support inclusion and meet the needs of individuals, offering a diverse range of play-based experiences. Young children should participate in decisions and actions affecting their outdoor play.

Provision for learning outdoors is responsive to the needs of very active learners, those who need sensory or language stimulation and those who need space away from others – it makes provision more inclusive and is a vital learning environment. When children's learning styles are valued, their self-image benefits. Boys, who tend to use active learning modes more than girls and until they are older, are particularly disadvantaged by limited outdoor play.

All children need full access to provision outdoors and it is important to know and meet the needs and interests of each child as an individual. Young children react differently to the spaces and experiences available or created so awareness and flexibility are key to the adult role. Observation and assessment (formative and summative), and intervention for particular support, must be carried out outside. While it is important to ensure the safety of all children, it is equally important to ensure all are sufficiently challenged.

Young children should take an active part in decisions and actions for outdoor provision, big and small. Their perspectives and views are critical and must be sought, and they can take an active role in setting up, clearing away and caring for the outdoor space.

The history of the Shared Vision and Values for Outdoor Play in the Early Years

Learning through Landscapes (LTL), the national school grounds and early years spaces organisation, has been the driving force behind the development of a strong vision about young children's access to outdoor experience for wellbeing and learning and a set of clearly articulated *'core values'* about what outdoor experiences should look and feel like, that is shared by the whole early years sector across England, Wales, Scotland and Northern Ireland.

In November 2003, LTL facilitated the bringing together of a wide range of early years specialists representing children, families and practitioners from Scotland, Wales and England and with high levels of expertise in quality outdoor provision for young children.

A remarkable level of common understanding and alignment about what mattered resulted in the launch and publication of a **Shared Vision and Values for Outdoor Play** in Nursery World magazine (1st April 2004) in poster format, also made available as a downloadable document on Learning through Landscape's website **www.ltl.org.uk**. The statements were intentionally made copyright-free to encourage their ongoing use and adaptation for a wide range of situations across the UK. During the initial promotion, thousands of educators, settings, parents and organisations endorsed the Vision and Values statements via LTL's website, adopting them for their own use. The **Early Years Vision and Values for Outdoor Play** formed part of the Early Years Foundation Stage guidance in 2008 to support the development of *'enabling environments'* outdoors (Department for Children, Schools and Families 2008) and have been published in several books on outdoor play (Warden 2005 & 2012, White 2007 & 2014, White 2011).

Participants in the Visions & Values Partnership work

Celia Burgess Macey, Goldsmiths, University of London
Diane Rich, Rich Learning Opportunities
Early Education
Early Excellence
Education Walsall
Forum for Maintained Nursery Schools and Children's Centres
Gill McKinnon, High School Yards Nursery School, Edinburgh
Grounds for Learning
Helen Tovey, University of Roehampton
Jan White, Early Childhood Natural Play

Kent EYDCP
Learning through Landscapes
Margaret Edgington
Marjorie Ouvry
Claire Warden, Mindstretchers
National Day Nurseries Association
Neath Port Talbot County Council
Nursery World magazine
Pre-School Learning Alliance
Sightlines Initiative

Opening Up The Outdoors - providing ongoing support

Valuing The Outdoors

The Core Values establish a base for understanding and thinking about being outdoors in the early years – providing firm foundations for moving forwards. These values are explored and illustrated extensively in the book, **Outdoor Provision in the Early Years** edited by Jan White (Sage, 2011).

As well as providing this value base for thinking about the outdoors, the **Opening Up the Outdoors** initiative includes two 'how to do it' strands that will help practitioners to provide learning through play outdoors that is rich, effective and satisfying – the **WHAT** and the **HOW** of really good outdoor play.

Unlocking Learning Outdoors – the WHAT of playing and learning outdoors

Unlocking Learning Outdoors is a structured framework, created by Jan White, which provides wide-ranging support for developing all aspects of outdoor provision and practice. Unlocking Learning Outdoors is a highly practical framework focusing on **WHAT** needs to be worked upon in order to fully harness the potential of the outdoors for young children's nurture, wellbeing, play, learning and development. Visit **www.earlychildhoodoutdoors.org** for information as this resource develops.

GATEWAYS to natural play – the HOW of playing and learning outdoors

Valuing The Outdoors is the 'master' booklet in a developing series of **GATEWAY** booklets produced through collaboration between Jan White (Early Childhood Outdoors) and Liz Edwards (Muddy Faces) to support the aims of the Opening Up The Outdoors initiative of more children thriving outdoors, more often and for longer, benefiting from richer and more meaningful environments offering authentic, rewarding and satisfying experiences.

Each of the **GATEWAY** booklets has a clear 'gateway' in provision and experience outdoors that it seeks to open. Each booklet offers a simple, straightforward and easy to implement aspect of development and action (such as making a mud kitchen), which actually opens up much more of the outdoors than at first meets the eye – providing a mud kitchen enables child driven play and gives access to deep exploration of both natural materials and human life.

Making a Mud Kitchen (White and Edwards 2011) is the first booklet in the Gateway series and is available as a free download from the Muddy Faces Outdoor Hub **www.muddyfaces.co.uk** Further booklets will address keystone provision such as playing with the rain, loose parts, woodwork and tools, den play and storytelling.

Opening each gate initiates a great way of harnessing the outdoors for enjoyable and worthwhile play and learning - contributing to opening up the full richness of playing and learning outdoors, and capturing the best the outdoors can provide for wellbeing, playing and learning. For ongoing information about Gateway booklets as they become available, visit the Outdoor Hub at **www.muddyfaces.co.uk**